# FAITH,
## *failure,*
# SUCCESS
#### VOLUME 4

I AM, I CAN

# I WILL

## J. ALISON

## JAIME A. GILL

## LIONEL HILAIRE

## KEISHA ROSE

## TOMMY DON TALLEY JR.

Cover Design: Janie Lott
Interior Design: Janie Lott
Published by: 220 Publishing

Faith, Failure, Success Volume 4: I Am, I Can, I Will.
J. Alison, Jaime A. Gill, Lionel Hilaire, Keiaha Rose and Tommy Don Talley Jr. First Edition.
ISBN: 978-1-6664-0431-9

# Acknowledgements

I want to publicly thank A'rianna McLean for wanting to know more about my story. What she thought was just an interview for her collegiate senior paper, was the beginning of me knowing that I needed to share more! Thank you for being an amazing young woman that consistently inspires me to boldly and unapologetically own and celebrate my unique journey of life! I am so proud of the woman you are and I hope that you too find that YOU ARE, YOU CAN, AND YOU WILL! God has so much in store for you! Let him continue to be your lamp and your guide.

— Jaime A. Gill

# Table of Contents

**I Will Overcome** *By Tommy Don Talley, Jr.*      **8**

**Hello, It's Me** *By Keisha Rose*      **16**

**When The Dream Is Not *The* Dream** *By J. Alison*      **32**

**I Will Leave A Legacy** *By Lionel Hilaire*      **46**

**The Perfect Shade of Lipstick** *By Jaime A. Gill*      **52**

# Foreword

**A**s we stand at the culmination of the remarkable journey that is the *Faith Failure Success* series, I find myself filled with a profound sense of pride and accomplishment. It is with immense satisfaction that we draw the curtain on this series, and I can confidently declare that we are concluding on the highest of notes. With "I am I can, and I will," we present to you not just a book, but a resounding call to action—a mission that beckons you to reclaim your life, reaffirm your presence in this world, and unabashedly demand all the goodness that it has to offer.

The pages of this book are a tapestry woven from the wisdom of some of our most seasoned and accomplished authors, as well as the fresh perspectives of talented newcomers. In harmonious symphony, their words give life to a companion piece that beautifully complements the other titles in our series: "Stories along the Entrepreneurial Journey," "Surviving the Storm," and "Turning Point." These books have collectively become beacons of insight, guiding countless individuals through challenges, inspiring their resilience, and illuminating the path to transformation.

This moment also calls for a heartfelt expression of gratitude. I extend my personal thanks to each and every author who lent their voice and story to this series. Your contributions have been nothing short of transformative, as you courageously delved into the depths of your experiences, unveiling facets of your journey even to those closest to you. In doing so, you have touched lives that you may never meet, sparking inspiration, kindling motivation, and effecting change simply by translating your thoughts into ink on these pages.

To you, our esteemed readers, I extend an invitation—an invitation to immerse yourselves in the pages of this edition and to embark on a journey of self-discovery and empowerment. As you do, I urge you to fortify your faith, for it is the bedrock upon which the grandest visions are built. Let the stories contained within these pages remind you that failure is but a fleeting moment, a stepping stone on the path to greatness. Your unique definition of success awaits your pursuit, one that resonates with your deepest desires and aspirations.

Should you find yourself seeking guidance, yearning for the spark to ignite your own transformation, look no further than the chapters of this book. Within them lie narratives of courage, determination, and triumph over adversity. By absorbing these tales, you will find the wellspring of courage to break free from whatever shackles have held you back. Just as the authors have shown through their narratives, you too possess the capacity to rise, to achieve, and to evolve into the best version of yourself.

In closing, let us celebrate the closing of one chapter and the opening of another. May the culmination of this series inspire you to venture forth with renewed vigor, unyielding faith, and an unquenchable thirst for success. Let the world witness your unwavering resolve to become the architect of your destiny. Remember, just as those who have penned their stories in these pages have proven time and again: You are enough, You can move forward , and you will succeed.

— Glenn Murray

# I Will Overcome

## BY TOMMY DON TALLEY JR.

*I consciously choose to be more than my scars, better than my mistakes, stronger than my pain & committed to my healing.*
*I Will Overcome.*

---

**A**s each day passes, I am reminded we are all just trying to make it through life. We all have stories about our lives, the good and the bad, and how they shaped who we are today. Life has taught me many lessons, and one of those is not giving my parents enough credit—this life stuff is hard. For all the ways they didn't do enough, I am reminded of the many ways they tried. Some people say they wish they could go back to being a kid again. I've thought of it, but I don't think life has beat me up enough to want to go back to my childhood. I didn't have the best childhood, in fact, my childhood still haunts me to this day.

As a father of three, I find myself lacking in certain areas my parents also did: patience, controlling my frustration and irritability, being understanding, and having unrealistic expectations. I see myself repeating those patterns, and I'm doing all I can to break the cycle. I am constantly challenged to be better than my parents; whether I'm in my head about it or it's said, I feel that pressure every day. To be a better parent to my kids and to provide them with everything I didn't have growing up. To ensure they aren't plagued by the same things I'm working endlessly to overcome. I don't want that for them. It must stop with me. It will stop with me.

Anyone who says being a parent is easy is lying; it is one of the hardest jobs out there. It's a non-stop job requiring you to be alert and one step ahead at all times. Despite numerous resources available on being a better parent, there is no perfect parent. There will be failures and successes, all of which are worth it if it means my kids are being raised in a happy and healthy environment.

## *Faith, Failure, and Success of Parenthood*

Each day, I consciously choose to be more than my scars, better than my mistakes, stronger than my pain, and committed to my healing. This allows me the space to be a committed, loving, vulnerable, and present husband and father. It's easy to get caught up in our failures as a parent. We often remember the bad times way more than we do our good ones. Maybe it's because we know that we are capable of being better—we know that we are more than our failures.

I'm far from being the perfect parent. I've made my mistakes. I still make mistakes today, far more than I should, unfortunately. We only know what we are used to; the only father I know how to be is the father that I had. If I'm going to be a better father it requires me to really be present with my family. It requires me to be honest with them about my thoughts, feelings, and actions. I need to be focused on the individual needs of my children, who are all unique.

It's easy to just go with the motions and let life run on autopilot. But that's how we stay in the cycles that we are in. It takes a lot to be present in our families' lives. We have busy lives filled with responsibilities and commitments; this makes us place our focus elsewhere instead of where it needs to be. I know I'm guilty of living on autopilot. I have a job that requires a lot of my time and effort, and it comes with a lot of responsibilities. When I go home after a hard day, I just want to relax and unwind. I don't want to think, I don't want noise, and a lot of the time, I don't want to talk. That's not always possible, especially when going home to my wife and three kids. But with the proper communication, our families can help us find ways to make a day better.

Being vulnerable to have open dialogues with my family about my feelings has been hard. Because with conversations come questions. How can I expect my kids to understand the reasons I am the way I am without asking questions about my childhood? I have to remind myself to be vulnerable, to open up and share my experiences. This is easier said than done; it's easy to let things stay the same, but it takes a strong commitment if you want to make things change.

My wife and kids may never understand why I am the way I am. Why I have the temper that I do, why I have the anger inside that I do, why it's so hard for me to be the parent I want to be. It's not that I don't want to change, but like I said earlier, I am the father that I had. Instead, I strive to be more like my heavenly father. God is love, compassion, strength, and forgiveness.

Faith has played an enormous role in my life. As a young boy, I learned to put my life in the hands of God, to turn my problems to Him knowing that he is my protector and provider and has my best interest at heart. Every day I faithfully pray to my heavenly father. I ask for His love, His wisdom, His patience, but most importantly, I ask that he keeps his hand on my family. God has truly done some amazing things in my family's life. Despite my many failures as a parent and husband, He has brought my family back to me and has kept them with me. We have learned to communicate more, to love more, to be more patient (most of the time).

Although I was raised in a Catholic church, it never really felt like I belonged there. We weren't very committed to our faith, so when I say I was raised in a Catholic church, I mean that we were baptized as babies and we went to church for funerals. Religion wasn't forced on me and my siblings, and I was OK with that. The first time I felt a relationship with God was at a church called Pilsen Assembly of God.

My mother and siblings would visit the church weekly, and when I would have visitations with her over the weekend, she would take us on Sundays. I didn't really understand what Pastor Andrew was saying; maybe I wasn't really paying attention to the word of God, and instead I was focused on my mom. It was at this point that I witnessed the love, hope, and forgiveness that God gave. I didn't quite understand it, but I knew what I was feeling was right.

I have seen my mom believe in something more those days. She showed me that despite our MANY failures, despite our mistakes and bad choices, despite our finances or living situations, we were loved. That's when I knew that my mom was trying; that's when I knew she was struggling. Struggling by living a life she didn't want, struggling by beating herself up for her mistakes and for her flaws. In return, God gave her what she needed. God gave her what every parent should give their children: love, hope, and forgiveness. Unconditionally.

Being a good parent requires faith, failures, and successes. Our failures don't define us. Our successes don't define us. But our faith—our faith is what makes us good parents. Faith that although things may be tough now, they won't always be this way. Faith that we can change our ways and be better. Faith that we can break these cycles that have plagued our families for generations. It stops with us; it stops now by making a conscious choice to push your family out of the hard times and into the life that we deserve. A life of love, hope, and forgiveness.

## *Breaking the Cycle*

*"Regardless of how weak or cracked my foundation was, it was always within my power to rebuild and create a solid foundation on which to live my life."* —Tommy Don Talley Jr.

I come from a long line of alcoholism, drug abuse, physical and verbal abuse, poor mental health, and premature death. My family seems as though we've been cursed; I wonder what my ancestors did to get my family to this point? Or perhaps the question should be, what didn't they do to bring us out of this toxic and deadly cycle? Surely my family would be much farther ahead had my ancestors handled these issues at the root. It takes a lot of love, hope, forgiveness, courage, and determination to break deadly cycles. To be honest, it's a lot of work to break these cycles, and at times, it seems way too out of reach. Giving up is the easy way out, and most of the time, it seems like the best option.

The hardest part about attempting to break these cycles is getting through the imposter syndrome. We know what we want to change, we know that we need to change, and we make the commitment to change. But what gets me the most is when I'm trying to be better but I can't. I can't be better 100% of the time, and I guess that's my expectation. When I can't be at my best, it causes me to fall back into this imposter mindset. "I'll never break these curses." "I'll never have control over my temper." "Maybe I'm not supposed to be a parent?" "It's silly to think I could overcome."

I can't let these thoughts win and take over my life. I have to be honest with myself and do what I can when I can. I will never be perfect, no one will. But as long as I hold on to my faith and stay determined, I know that eventually my hard work will produce better results. My family will be happier, healthier, more blessed, more loved, and cherished more, as they deserve.

This multigenerational cycle of abuse and addiction stops with me. I possess the tools and motivation to break free and heal from my childhood. I know I deserve to heal from the pain, overcome the trauma, and remember I'm worthy of good things. My family is worthy of change, worthy of love, worthy of forgiveness. In years to come, my family will see change.

We will overcome.

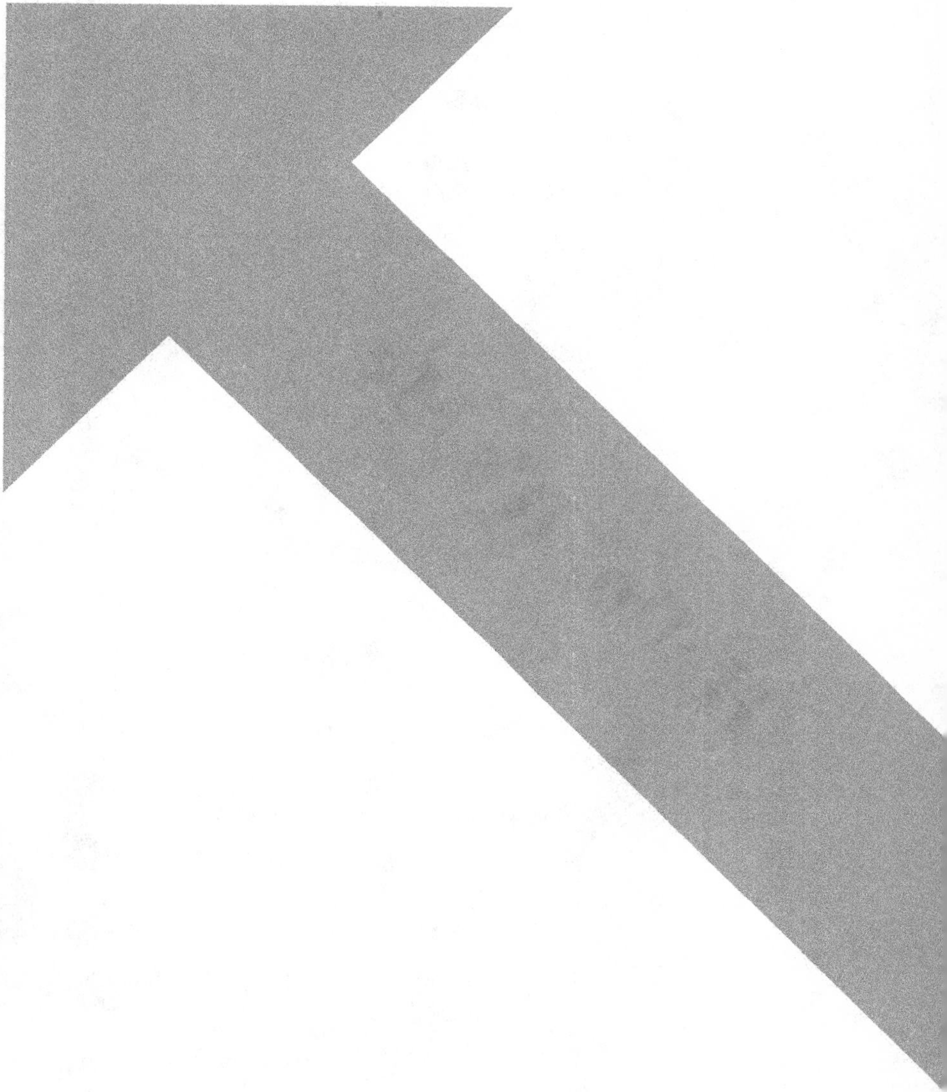

# Hello, It's Me

## BY KEISHA ROSE

*I just knew that writing my contribution piece to Faith, Failure, & Success would be effortless because the "I AM" is part of my brand; it's what I have been standing in the mirror and writing on sticky notes for years, saying to myself. When Glenn said that he wanted me to be a part of this edition of FFS, I was like, "no problem, I can write that in five minutes." Let me just say that I am Keisha Rose, and I am a liar. Like so many writers, I became speechless and I couldn't get my thoughts together, so I pushed it to the side because I'm an actress, a businesswoman, and an entrepreneur; I got this! NOPE! I'm a woman that wears many hats, but when it comes to sitting down and dealing with myself, that part is hard. You see, I'm a complicated woman—not in a negative or hard-to-deal-with way, but I'm my biggest opponent, and even I can't stop me on my best day, so here we go, my chapter of FFS: I Am—I Can—I Will...Thank You Glenn Murray for believing in me!*

---

## *I AM...*

"I Am" are the two most important words that you would ever say to yourself; you are manifesting whatever words that you put after it to shape your reality. I've lived by the power of this. I believe in it so much that it is now part of my brand, so I must believe in it, right?

I was born LaKeisha on the West Side of Chicago to a young single mother who worked very hard. We've always had very nice things; I don't remember at any time being hungry or without any necessities. My mother had a great support system. I grew up with my aunts, uncles, and grandmother, and my cousins were like my siblings. I was very smart in school and grew up thinking that I could be anything that I wanted to be, and I knew that I didn't want to stay in the city for my entire life. I knew that there was so much more for me to do, for me to become, and sometimes that requires you to move away from everything and everybody. You have to become uncomfortable in order to grow. I've never believed in fairy tales, prince charming, fairy godmothers, and that BS that they make you read and believe in as a child; growing up in the city makes you quickly realize that you're not going to run off with a prince or live in a castle. Now, in order to leave the city, the only home I've ever known, I need to work hard, get good grades, keep my head low, and survive the city streets, and please don't get this wrong: it's not where you live, it's how you live.

The West Side of Chicago has some beautiful neighborhoods and some of the best people, but the part that I lived in was surrounded by gangbangers and drug dealers, but back then in those days they looked out for the neighborhoods, and they made sure that we went to school and that we were safe. I remember one day I was trying to ditch school and one of the gang leaders yelled at me, "Aren't you supposed to be at school? Let's go, I'm walking you to the bus stop. Get your butt to school or I'm telling your mama." He had some nerve, but they looked out for me and my mom who worked nights. Crazy, right? But there was an order within the gang life, a street code; no unnecessary shootings, nothing like today. My mother was and is a beautiful woman who had never brought home anybody; she never had "friends." It was just me and her until she met "The Monster" and decided to marry him. Children are blessed with the sense of recognizing "bad people," and I knew from day one that there was something evil about him, but she seemed happy, so I didn't speak up. I was only around seven years old at the time or younger.

Have you ever looked into the eyes of the devil? I have! He had three kids from his previous marriage, but I knew and felt immediately that I was never going to be treated like he treated his kids. My biological father was married to his wife and my two sisters lived with them; they lived in Mississippi, so I had little to no contact with him until I started going down south every year to visit my grandmother and great-grandmother. The Monster was very controlling and physically abusive to my mother. I witnessed so much of his rage towards her, and she would still put on her makeup, take care of me, and manage to go to work. My mother is the strongest woman that I know; she is a proud southern woman with the most beautiful spirit and a smile to match, but she was probably dying on the inside, now thinking back. It's amazing what a woman goes through while always managing to make her child or children feel like everything is OK. The first thing an abuser will do is isolate you from your family and friends in order to gain mind control over their victims, and they will start telling people how big of a liar you are, so that when you start telling your truth, no one will believe you.

I was taught from a very early age how to be silent and scared, how to keep secrets, how to lie, and how to smile even when I was broken.... after many years of that monster's physical abuse to my mother, he made a choice to turn his evil up a notch by setting his eyes on me. All little girls should be innocent, safe, and protected in their home, and that was all taken away from me, but I was determined not to let his evil ways kill my spirit. How did people not notice this broken little girl? Or was I that good at pretending? It's amazing to me how your childhood traumas will affect and shape the outcome of your life; that's why I don't believe in telling people to "get over it." How can I tell you to get over something when I don't know where your pain comes from and how deep it is?

After years of abuse, it took me a long time to trust people, and I also made bad choices in men, but with years of prayer and therapy, I found myself, and I found my happiness again. Entertainment through film, TV, and music is what got me through some difficult days. Music was and is my first love. My mother would play music every Saturday or Sunday, and I would sing the lyrics and study the chorus and the album credits. I wanted to know about the band, the writer of the songs, and the background singers. Music is the soundtrack of my life. I have a song for every season of my life, even for the bad things that happened to me. Film/TV is my happy place, my joy, if you will. I would imagine myself on TV or on a stage memorizing and saying monologues since I was nine years old, pretending to be someone else or being somewhere else got me through my trauma. I had my Emmy acceptance speech down, I knew it by heart I also practiced signing my autograph on every piece of paper in the house, so there was no giving up on me and what I could become. I saw it, therefore I believed it.

The day that I decided that I was NOT defined by my abuse any longer or my past is the day that Keisha Rose was born. HEEEEYYYY I AM not my scars. I AM brave. I AM resilient. I AM Strong. I Am not what happened to me, I am what I choose to become, so let me reintroduce myself to you. I am Keisha Rose: Actress, Model, Writer, Producer, Director, Co-Owner of G-Rose Productions, and CEO of the I AM Collections by Keisha Rose. I could have taken that abused part of my life and used it as an excuse to not become anything and just feel sorry for myself, but I knew GOD had a special assignment in and on my life. I chose to be happy, educated, successful, and to love others despite the trauma.

Statistically, I should be uneducated, on welfare, working a minimum wage job or no job at all, living in government housing, and never dreaming of becoming BIGGER, but we all know the phrase "the devil is a liar." I Am more than a conqueror, I AM becoming....Oh! I'm sure you guys want to know what happened to "The Monster." Well...I finally spoke up. The little girl said "no more." I wrote a letter to my friend, and thank GOD my friend gave the letter to his mother, and she called my mother. I called her two years ago to thank her; she was unaware of how she literally saved my life. I pray that mother never blames herself for his actions, because she will always be my hero. She was a victim herself. Remember, he controlled the house. My mother is now married to an amazing man. She now knows what true love feels like.

Typically, in Black households, this becomes the family's secret, and it is dealt with within the family—no counseling, no sitting down at the table to talk, no time to heal, just move on. The crazy part is that everyone in my family knew that it happened, but nobody ever asked me about it or asked me, "how are you doing?" Nothing at all. Let's break that generational curse!! Honestly, I'm not sure what happened to him. I came home one day, and he was no longer there, and he was never mentioned again. I was finally free. I had to forgive him and wish him well; if not I would be stuck, and I wouldn't be where I am today. Forgiveness is a powerful thing. The trauma was not my fault, but my healing was all on me....I AM HEALED. This girl from the West Side had stitched herself back together, put herself through college, and dreamed of a life in entertainment, and guess what...**DREAMS DO COME TRUE!**

## *I CAN...*

*I can be just as powerful as I am because this is giving yourself permission to be.* God told me as a young girl that I would be an "entertainer," but I didn't know to what capacity or how. I was a skinny, tall girl throughout grade and high school, and I was so much taller than all of my friends. In grade school, we had to line up by height, and I was always in the back; this drove me crazy. My self-esteem and self-confidence were so low that I would walk with a slouch so that I could appear shorter to blend in. My group of friends were in the front of the line, so I felt so isolated, and I would cry when I got home. I came home the same as usual, crying and upset, and one day my mother said to me, "Stand up straight; you're tall and that's OK."

I woke up one Saturday morning to my mother saying, "Get dressed; you have an appointment." I got dressed and we drove to downtown Chicago. See, back in the day, going downtown was a privilege; the architecture of the buildings, the skyline, the movie theaters, the museums, the lights, the restaurants were all breathtaking. The city itself is a character, and the people were always moving so fast. I couldn't be still sitting on the passenger side of my mom's black four door 1988 Cutlass Supreme; I was so excited. We pulled up to these two corn on the cob-looking buildings (Marina City) surrounded by the river. I walked in and I couldn't believe my eyes. I saw a group of tall, beautiful girls everywhere; some were six feet tall or more. My mother had signed me up for modeling classes, and OMG, I felt like I belonged. I wasn't the tallest girl in the room anymore; immediately a boost of confidence came over me, and it was over.

My modeling coach was Ms. Kennedy, a tall older lady, sophisticated with her hair sandy brown touching her shoulders, and she was beautiful with long beautiful nails, and she wore this velvet maroon lipstick (it's funny the things that you remember about a person). She taught me how to walk with my head up, how to fix my face, how to give attitude without being attitude-ish, how to use my long legs with grace, how to use my big eyes as I passed you by, and that turn at the end of the runway—you couldn't tell me nothing. I had on heels, which I would never have worn in the past because they would make me so much taller, but I fell in love with them and myself that day. I was soon in all the fashion shows and from there went on to model for more people. I even got booked for a  local modeling TV show here in Chicago. Ms. Kennedy called me because she wanted to get me in a local magazine. I could not believe it; what could be better than this? As life would have it, I couldn't do the shoot for the major magazine because the one thing that my mother feared for me was now happening. I was pregnant and finally a statistic as another teenage pregnant girl. I worked so hard not to become a part of that group, but, yep, that was now my reality. I felt so defeated; I was so disappointed in myself, and the look on my mother's face told me exactly how she felt about it. So my mother, who was my world, gave me two options at that point: get an abortion so I could continue this journey that I was on, or keep it, but I couldn't stay in my mother's house with a baby. How in the hell do you decide something like that at seventeen years old?

Years later, I met this music producer (yep, I have some music floating around somewhere), and I was in a girl group called "New Era." That same producer knew a guy working on a film, and he asked if I wanted to audition for a role, WTH! I didn't have the first clue about how to audition for a movie. We got to the audition, and the director gave me a sheet of paper and asked me to read it while he recorded me. This was totally different from modeling and from being in the studio behind a microphone, but thought, I CAN do this. I read the lines, and then I read them again, some words I delivered without the paper. I have a great memory; I can look at something and remember it, so I read it again, and he said, "Thank you, we'll be in touch." We got in the car, drove off to get something to eat, and the producer called and said, "Can you come back to read with the lead actor in the film?" We went back in, me and the lead male actor read our lines together, and once again, "Thank you, we'll be in touch." I got it!!!! I got a lead role in my first movie, which did well financially with Maverick Films, so you see how one thing leads to another and open doors for others if you allow yourself to be open to new possibilities. I would have missed all of that if I was not confident in myself enough to take on new challenges and opportunities. Here's a hint: the producer and director of my first film is now one of our business partners today for our production company. GOD put the people that I would need in my life—a full circle moment for me.

Coming off the success of my first movie, I was offered another film, and from there I knew that film/entertainment was what I wanted to do. I loved how I felt after getting a script, memorizing it, being on set ALL DAY and NIGHT; if you can do something all day or for free and still have joy while doing it, that's what you should be doing. I was studying everything: the cameraman, the audio person, the actors, the PAs, the ex-tras— everything. I went to acting school and studied under the famous Ted Sarantos, and continued until he closed his studio; you can never stop learning and studying your craft. I now have over twenty movie credits as a producer, writer, and director to my name. I also have two Atlanta actor awards. I allowed myself permission to do all these things, and I did not limit myself. "I CAN do anything" became my new normal. I no longer said no when it came to my career in the film/entertainment industry;

I said YES and learned it if I didn't know how to do it. Did you guess which option I took from my mother?

## *I WILL…*

I will hold you accountable for you. Saying that you will do or commit to something is giving your word, and we all know that your word is bond. It's obvious that you cannot be successful without having some faith, but it comes with its share of failures. I've had my childhood traumas, I've had many heartbreaks and pain, I've had my struggles and hard times, but I've always had my Faith. I can honestly say that I wouldn't be who I am today if I had not gone through any of them. I've had to do some serious healing. Healing is a practice, it's ongoing, are you ever really 100% healed? Probably not, but you have to be 100% committed to healing for it to work.

Forgiveness is ongoing. If I did not put in the work to heal from any of my trauma, I would have put my pain and trauma on other people. I had to decide that was what I wanted to do and then actively do it. I had to go to counseling and for a long time I was ashamed of what I went through—that's crazy, right? I was the victim, yet I was ashamed. I never wanted to talk about it. Little Keisha didn't believe in fairytales. I now believe in them because I have made my dreams come true, and when you really think about fairy tales, it's all about the happy ending of the story, right? Well, it was me and GOD that decided how my life would turn out. I am now in a place where I believe in Prince Charming, happily ever after, and a dream job or jobs. I now believe that you can have it all.

Do you know that you are Worthy? Deserving? Enough? Of all the manifestations that you bring to yourself. I hear a lot of people blaming their childhood for their lives now. "I can't get a job because my mother did this or that." "I can't have a healthy relationship because he or she did this or that." The easy part is not trying; the easy part is walking away or giving up on something that you asked or prayed for. We let fear come into our psyche and we talk ourselves out of something great because the "great" is unfamiliar. If you are reading this, stop running, stop interfering with your greatness, and stop sabotaging your happiness. You are meant to do amazing things; you deserve to love and to be loved. If you are willing to fight for your greatness and your happiness, you will keep it—not only keep it, but appreciate it. Speak over your life with I AM, I CAN, and I WILL and watch GOD move in ways that will blow your mind. You will surprise yourself with all the greatness that is within you. I almost missed out on so many amazing opportunities that were meant for me because I didn't know my own worth.

Today, as I write this, I AM continuing to grow on so many levels. I am the best version of me. I am still growing and learning my acting skills, still learning how to produce and direct a great show, and finally, how to write a great script. My goal is to get a production deal or a first look deal for original content on a major network. We want to introduce new content along with new and upcoming actors/actresses with all our projects. Films were introduced to me as a little girl by my mother, and I've imagined myself on that big screen since then. Yes! I've manifested it into my life: the lights, the scenery, the actors, the movement of it all. Some people want to be famous, and if that's your goal, you're in the film business for the wrong reasons. Film and Entertainment is a 24/7 marriage. It's hard work: it's networking, it's studying and forever learning, it's something that you have to do every day without apologizing for it. Most importantly, it's many days of sacrifices, which includes your family, holidays, and friends. It's an isolated feeling, but you have to keep going anyways. It's being rejected over and over one minute, and the next minute, you are back at it with the same passion every time. You must be intentional in your movements, be purposeful with every meeting, and by all means necessary, always be prepared and use your discernment when it comes to opportunities and people. I'm not meant to be in everyone's project or film, and that's OK with me.

You see certain people in everybody's projects because they just want to be seen and they don't really care about the project; they won't even promote the film. They are on to the next project just to appear to look busy, but busy doesn't mean productive. I take my time and pick what's best for me at that moment. I ask myself what I can bring to this film and if I connect with the character or the script, and if my answer is no, that's what it is. We have to remember that people don't go to the movies to see you, they go to the movies to see themselves and what they are going through in that moment in the film (read that again). Looking back as I write this, I thank GOD for the hard times. I am no longer afraid, worried, or easily intimidated by anyone or anything. I've had the people closest to me tell me to give it up and that I will not become anything. I had to remove these people from my life because they had a direct passage to my psyche; eventually I would've started to believe them and navigate in that space. I had to learn to use my voice. I speak up for myself now because little Keisha was silenced. I will continue to use it through my scripts or through my production. My voice will be HEARD!

*I dedicate this to every little girl that was silenced. You are special, you are loved and protected. You matter and your trauma is not your fault! Use your voice! Speak up!*

*I also dedicate this to my son Alex. I chose you! We had to grow up together and I thank you for being my biggest supporter and my reason for working so hard. Love, your mom!*

*To my mother: thank you for showing me what hard work looks like, for showing me what dedication looks like, and, finally, for showing me what love and sacrifice looks like! Love you!*

*To little Keisha: I'm proud of you! You've survived too many storms to ever let raindrops stop you! You are a survivor! Keep going and shine. Remember, GOD will send everything and everybody you will need to become successful!*

Every person has a story; what's yours? What's your IAM?

In closing, I will leave you with this, and I hope that I've helped someone to never give up on themselves, and to use your voice: somebody is depending on your story. If this little skinny, tall, awkward little girl from the West Side of Chicago can do it, you can, too!

# *I Am Enough…*

*I am enough on my worst day when I don't feel like getting out of bed. I Am enough, even when my heart has been broken. I am enough when I have to cover up the hurt and I feel like paint peeling off the walls. I am enough when I look in the mirror and see scars instead of beauty marks. I am enough when I'm exhausted and didn't complete any tasks or deadlines that day. I am enough when I've auditioned for films or pitched an idea to a network and it was rejected. I am enough when everything is falling apart around me and I feel like a failure. You are enough, and no matter what, you will always be enough. Give yourself grace, be kind and gentle to you, and most importantly, believe in yourself!...Keisha Rose* 🌷

# When the Dream is Not the Dream

## BY J. ALISON

# The Inspiration

"Hold your ear." I winced as my mother blew on the hot comb before gliding it through my nappy hair. I would pray the sizzle of the fiery hot comb wouldn't burn my scalp. Ooowee, I couldn't wait for her to get done. It was pure torture every other Saturday morning to sit in that kitchen next to the stove and smell burning hair for an hour. Hurry up, tenth birthday! In our house, when you turned ten, you could get a hair relaxer, which meant bye bye hot comb. All the house rules that I hated: you couldn't get a relaxer until you were ten, you couldn't date until you were sixteen, and the phone was unplugged every night at bedtime. Oh, and let's not forget, when you became a teenager and started going out with your friends, you had to be in by 10:00 PM. And absolutely NO calls from boys! It's no wonder I ran away from home on my sixteenth birthday.

There was one fun pastime at our house every weekend, and that was my mother's beauty shop in the basement. Every Saturday morning, except on Hot Comb Saturdays, I would lay in the bed and listen to all the juicy gossip rising through the floor vent. My mom had this friend named Lillie who was always complaining about her new husband's six kids from a previous marriage and how they never had any money because of his child support payments. She was hilarious. When they started talking low, I would walk downstairs and go into the shop and sit and listen. To this day, I don't understand why my mother never told me to leave 'cause it was grown folks' business, but she didn't. From ten years of age until I got married at eighteen (I know—dumb), I grew up watching my mother do hair in our basement. She graduated from a kitchen beautician to a licensed cosmetologist, which made me want to be just like her but on a much bigger scale. It took me a long time to get there. I was well past my forties when I did it, but I went to school, graduated with my bachelor's in business management, and opened my first full-service salon. I was so proud of myself. My mother had a one-chair salon in the basement, which was a great accomplishment for someone who had to quit school in eleventh grade, get a job, and take care of her younger siblings while her mother recuperated in a hospital from a near-fatal car accident. My salon was a ten-chair salon with five spa rooms, an office, a private shower, and a full-service kitchen. It was the biggest salon in the tri-county area. Had I only known the dream was not "the dream," I would have done things so differently.

## The Cliff

After running my salon for two years, I decided to open a second one a couple of towns over. To this day, that decision was one of my biggest mistakes in business. My primary salon was literally bleeding money monthly, nowhere near breaking even. The decision to open a second one was disastrous. Although the second salon was for men only, much smaller, and only a $10,000 start-up, it soon became another liability. Each month, I was slowly draining my savings to stay afloat. There's a saying in business when you need to go up higher: "Sometimes you have to jump off the cliff and grow wings on the way down." I had no idea my cliff was on its way.

One evening around 7:00 PM, after closing the salon, I'm driving to the bank to drop off some money in the night deposit box, and my phone rings. It's my girlfriend Livy. I answer, and she sounds super excited.

"Hey girl, are you busy?"

"No, just dropping some money off in the night deposit. What's up?"

"I have this friend who is looking for a seventh person to join their DBO Enterprise to replace a salon owner who dropped out at the eleventh hour. There are seven of them who are closing a deal together this week, and they need an answer tonight for the salon slot. It's a salon and spa opportunity in the Detroit airport."

My heart instantly began racing. "Who do I need to talk to about it and what are the requirements to become a partner?"

"I don't know. You will have to talk to my guy friend who is the president of the company. He's in Paris and wants to talk to you tonight if you're available. I told him I would let him know."

Thoughts were going through my mind at warp speed. "OK, give me his number and I'll call him."

"No, he told me to let the person know, and he would call them at 9:00PM sharp."

"OK, give him my number."

"OK girl, I told him you would be great for this opportunity. Make sure you're by the phone. His name is Samuel Levings."

"I will be, and thank you so much, Livy!"

I hit "end call," and my heart was still racing. I wondered what I would need to do to get in on this deal? Wow! A salon in an airport! That's a freakin' GOLD MINE!

It's 9:00PM, and my phone rings. "Hello?"

"Yes, this is Samuel Levings. Is this June?"

"Yes, how are you sir?"

"I'm fine, thanks for asking. I'm assuming Livy told you why I'm calling, correct?"

"Yes, but she said you would finish filling me in on everything."

"Correct. What we have here is a wonderful opportunity to join a DBO group without having to go through the red tape of application and airport concession approval through Detroit Metro. You would essentially be replacing someone who deserted without notice. It's a golden opportunity."

He continued to explain the entire business model along with airport concession fees, and then "it" showed up. That cliff I mentioned earlier. The one that I would need to jump off. At the end of his spiel, he lowered the boom. "Oh, and you will need $65,000 to join, which must be paid by Friday. My assistant, Olga, will call you tomorrow via Skype. She will give you the entire salon breakdown as it relates to annual revenue, quarterly airport fees, current employee count, payroll, etc. The current staff is on autopilot, but you'll need to be at the salon at least one day a week. It's also up to you if you want to keep the current staff or hire your own. Olga will also tell you how the money needs to be wired."

At that very moment, I froze. All my excitement vanished. I just sat there staring at the cliff. Fear began to take over and I couldn't jump. He asked me a question, and I replied, "Huh?"

"Can you take a call tomorrow afternoon around 2:00 central time from my assistant?"

"Uh, yes."

"Do you have Skype downloaded on your computer? Because if not, you will need to get that downloaded before the call."

"Yes, I already have it, no problem."

"Great, I will pass your information on. Have a good evening."

"Yes, you too."

I went to bed that night thinking, how can I withdraw $65,000 out of my savings and continue to run my salons? I will be flat broke in a few months. I laid awake thinking for hours until I finally drifted off to sleep.

The alarm clock starts ringing, and I roll over and shut it off. It's 7:00AM. It felt like I had only been asleep for minutes, but it was time to get up, get ready and head to the salon. $65,000. I can't pay that, I thought as I was stepping into the shower. I have it, but I just can't take that kind of risk. I'll have to close my salons because the Detroit salon will take all my money to run. I can't possibly do this. I was slowly but surely talking myself out of the best opportunity I had ever had in business. I finished showering, got dressed, and headed to the salon.

It was a typical day. Customers coming and going. Stylists chatting it up with each other and having fun talking to their customers. A month ago, my receptionist quit, and none too soon, because I couldn't afford to pay her anymore. I was now the receptionist and the cleaning service for the salon. The day seemed to fly by. I looked up at the clock, and it was time to go home and get ready for the call from Paris. I drove home, ran into the house, and set up my laptop on the coffee table.

It's 2:00PM and the Skype call begins to ring. Wow! She's punctual. "Hello! How are you?"

"You are June, yes?"

"Yes."

"Nice to meet you. My name is Olga. I will be explaining the entire process to you to become a member of our group."

Olga looked to be in her late twenties, blonde with a thick foreign accent. As she was explaining everything, I was sitting there trying to figure out how I was going to tell this woman I didn't have the money but still wanted to be a part of the group. When she was finished with her presentation, including emailing me all the stats and financial reports from the salon, I made my biggest "hood" move ever. I asked could they "front" me the money and I would pay them back out of the salon's revenue? She looked at me like I was crazy and tried to contain herself. She was so kind at a time when she could have completely insulted me for being so naïve. She replied, "I doubt it, but I will check and get back to you."

I never heard from Olga or Samuel again. Oh, and by the way, did I mention, the airport salon's annual gross revenue was 1.2 million? Yeah...big mistake. When fear takes the place of logic, you don't even think straight. All rationality leaves you. I'd convinced myself I would go broke right after hearing the salon rakes in 1.2 million dollars a year! I was looking at the two little salons I had fearing I would lose them when all along, God was trying to save them and give me more than I ever imagined. All the devil wants to do is trick you, and he uses fear to do it.

I went back to the salon feeling relieved, but little did I know that that decision would haunt me for years.

## A Time of Discovery

It had now a full two years after the airport opportunity, and the salon was on life support. After closing my second salon six months earlier, I was faced with the decision of how to tell all my employees, right before Thanksgiving, that they were no longer going to have a place to work. I couldn't bear the thought of looking in their faces with the bad news, so I chose a conference call instead. I decided I would tell everyone on a Saturday night after the salon was closed so they could have Sunday and Monday to get over the shock since we were closed those days. I will never forget the silent cries over the phone line when I told everyone I had no other choice but to close the salon. After I made the announcement, I told them I would let them purchase any equipment they needed out of the salon at a ridiculous discount to help them relocate. No one spoke, only cried. So I ended the call.

The next few weeks were extremely sad. But in every death, there's always a birth. You just have to recognize it. As each stylist broke the news to their clients, some began to cry in the chair. I had no idea the impact we made on the lives of so many women. During these final weeks, women began opening up to me about how the salon was their respite. They started telling me what they were going through, and I began to counsel them. Most of our clients wanted to follow the stylists to their new location. They were shocked when I gave the new addresses of many, because in this business, owners don't help stylists become profitable somewhere else. Many required their staff to sign a "none compete" clause upon hiring. But not me. I don't believe in blocking one's blessings. So, let's get to the reason for this story. When something falls apart through no fault of your own, it may be because you need to go in a different direction. God is moving you into your purpose. A door closes, jobs terminate, and businesses don't work because you never should have been in that position in the first place. Allow God to take you where you are "supposed to be" and stop trying to be where you "want to be." Your purpose is supported by your gifts. Not your talents. There's a difference. Anyone can learn a talent. You can go to school and develop a talent. But a "gift"–that's from God. And it's in you from the day you are born. James 1:17 says, "Every good gift and every perfect gift is from above, and cometh down from the Father of lights, with whom is no variableness, neither shadow of turning." I had a gift to prophecy since I was born. It began showing up in my teens, but I really didn't understand the depth and weight of it until several years later. It never occurred to me—the reason people always came to me for answers was my prophetic gift. Over time, I became more and more accurate in prophesizing and began realizing what God had placed in me and who I really was. I thought my dream was to become a wealthy salon owner, but the dream really wasn't "the dream". You must discover your true purpose, and God is the only one who can reveal that to you.

During the salon's last week, women kept coming to the front desk and telling me how much they appreciated me and what the salon meant to them. I was floored. You never know how you affect people, which is why it's so important to treat everyone right no matter how they treat you. They wanted to stay in touch, and some connected with me on Facebook and made personal phone calls after the salon closed. Then something unexpected happened. One afternoon, during a lunch break, the Lord spoke to me and said, Turn your prophetic gift into a business. I was like, What? Turn it into a business? Never once did I think about monetizing the counsel I had been giving for years. The word of God says in Proverbs 18:16—"'A man's gift maketh room for him, and bringeth him before great men.'" The translation of that passage is that your gift is designed to create an economy for you. It's designed to make money, which will take you places you never could have imagined.

I began building my client base by offering free prophetic advisement sessions. Soon after, I started charging $35 for a forty-five minute session. People were blown away at the accuracy of what I was releasing in the session about their private lives. The session would start out with prophecy and end with advisement. The sessions were held on a conference line, and oftentimes halfway through the prophecy segment, I could hear the person crying. I was just as shocked as they were at the accuracy of what was coming out of my mouth. I realized this thing was truly God and not me. As time went on, I increased my price to $75 per session. The salon had been closed for a year, and I went back to working in corporate, which I hated. However, my prophetic advisement business kept growing. Then another instruction from God came, and this time it was something I NEVER would have dreamed of. He said, Get on Facebook and start teaching.

The following Monday night at 7:30PM, I got on. It took me almost ten minutes to push the start button to go live. I was so nervous! I must have fidgeted and re-fixed my hair ten times before pushing the button. I finally hit "Go Live," and before I knew it, my pitch was the level of hollering. LOL! Nervous energy will make you do crazy stuff. But when I ended, someone I had never met before sent me a DM telling me how accurate I was with the prophetic word. It was so encouraging. And with that, "Monday Night Live!" was born. Each week, I became calmer, until I finally could push the Go Live button soon after I sat down in front of the computer. One time during a broadcast, one of my close friends texted me saying, "June, that background noise has got to go!" At first, I didn't catch on, but then I looked at the raggedy curtains behind me and started laughing. I was broadcasting in our cabana out back and it was a little ratchet, so I purchased a backdrop and hung it.

I had been broadcasting for months when I received an in-box message from one of my viewers named Pam asking if she could speak with me via phone. I called her, and we instantly clicked. I prophesized to her about her career and her personal life. As time went on, we became great friends. Turns out, she has the gift of prophecy as well. She started encouraging me to go higher in my prophetic advisement business. Her first piece of advice was about my fee. She said it was way too low. I cringed at the thought of increasing it from $75. One of my professors once told me, "People will pay for what they value. Your product must be priced at the value it holds. No client will pay $500 for breast augmentation, no matter how remarkable the doctor claims the product is." I never forgot that. It was time for me to put it to the test. I increased my price to $100 per session. People paid it without hesitation. I realized the value was worth more, and I increased the fee to $250 for a forty-five minute session. Clients continued to pay. In addition to my prophetic advisement, I started offering an online dream interpretation class. It was a five-week self-directed program. None of this could have been possible without my prophetic gift. You must discover "who you are." You must find your purpose and begin to position yourself there. Monday Night Live began to grow. In addition to Facebook, people started tuning in via YouTube. After closing out one night, I looked at my stats and stared when I saw 85 people had shared my broadcast and over 400 people were on live! I was stunned! I decided to begin an online ministry, and I named it J. A. Journey Consulting. I wanted it to encapsulate every gift—dream interpretation, prophetic advisement, prophecy classes, and ministry. And just think, none of this happened until AFTER my salons failed.

I will end with this: the death of one thing is always the birth of another. Hold your head up when everything falls apart, because you're on your way to your God-given purpose. I moved from Illinois to Texas and am now currently looking for a building in Dallas to open a school of ministry. And here is the cherry on top. A friend called me one morning at 6:30 AM while I was getting ready for work and said, "God told me to tell you you missed an opportunity, but He's bringing it back around again." I held my head down and started to cry. I thought the airport opportunity was gone for good. God is a good God. Jeremiah 29:11 says, "I know the thoughts I think towards you. Thoughts of peace and not of evil, to give you a good end."

God is the sole architect of your future, and your future is destined to be great.

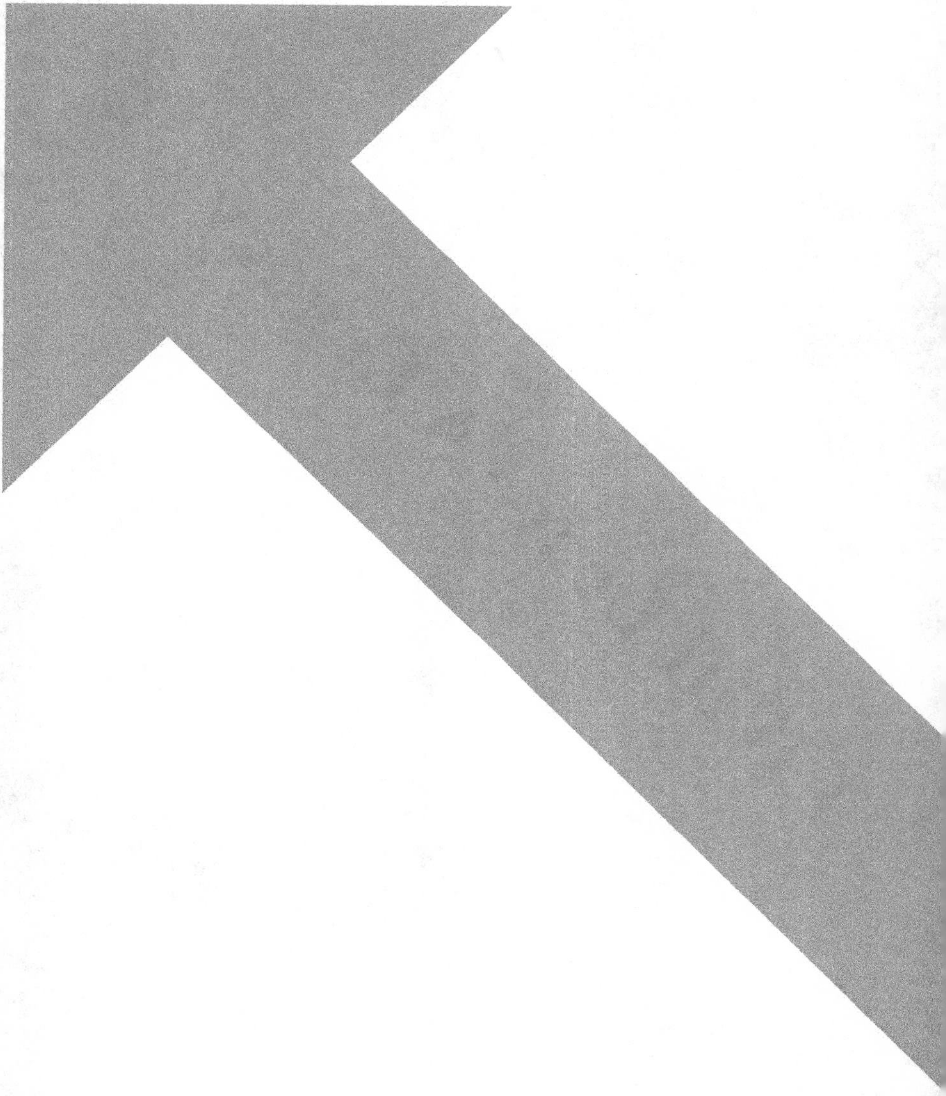

# I Will Leave A Legacy

## BY LIONEL HILAIRE

*I'm a thug and a playa....*

**B**eing born and raised in the city of Fort Lauderdale wasn't the worst place I could've been, but it wasn't the greatest, either.

From the time I was a young boy, there was a burning desire in me to be rich, look good, and have nice things. I began the journey by observing my surroundings to find inspiration. To find something and/or someone I can imitate.

I turned on the television. The news had males who resembled me in the streets robbing banks and taking lives. On the entertainment channels, they told me that the successful men like myself were rappers, drug dealers, and playas.

Then I looked at the billboards. There were two types of men who looked like me. One was wanted for murder. The other: his family and the law were searching for justice because he had been murdered.

Then I got a revelation....I'm a thug and a playa! This must be who I am, I thought to myself.

Quickly, I took another look at my surroundings. I sure didn't want to take a person's life, and I did not want to rob a bank, but...I wanted to look like a thug. And I wanted to be a playa. The guy that has multiple women desiring him and wanting him.

Now, in order for me to become that guy, I had to cultivate it. I began to watch more music videos that inspired my revelation. Walked my neighborhood and intentionally walked down the streets where the drug dealers lived. I got closer to the males who sagged their pants.

Yes, I'm a great student! My underwear was showing. I incorporated cuss words in my vocabulary, and the way I walked changed from a nerd to a more brave-looking and dangerous appearance. It was working!

This went on from about grades six to twelve. During those years, I tried drugs and alcohol, and at age thirteen, I had intercourse for the first time.

During grade twelve, something hit me. I glanced back over the years and thought to myself, this isn't who I really am. Deep down, I knew my parents didn't raise me like this. They didn't swear, nor did they allow us to swear in our home.

My parents didn't listen to degrading music. They didn't drink alcohol or smoke. At that very moment, I became frustrated and depressed. I'd built a life of a lie around me. I'd cultivated a community around myself that potentially could lead me to premature death, and that wasn't a great feeling at all!

This was not how I wanted to be remembered.

Then a great distraction happened! The girl I met in summer of 1999 had become pregnant with my child. The pregnancy gave me an excuse and an escape from the life I built.

I called the pregnancy a great distraction because I believe it saved my life and took my focus away from the wrong things and people. Having a child put me in focus. I began to walk and talk differently because now I had a little version of myself to care after.

Today, I have four beautiful children—Kyla, Chelsea, Syleena and Lionel Jr.—and the same young lady I met in summer of

1999 is the mother of all four. Not just that: she is my wife of over seventeen years.

We have a nonprofit organization called Divine Potential Services, Inc. 501c3. Our mission is Restoring Families. Empowering Change. We became the organization we desperately needed in our time of need. We've served the South Florida area by hosting events for families in financial, relational, and other crises Black families face in our communities since 2016.

My earlier years began a little rough and my name wasn't the greatest in my neighborhood. However, things have changed for the better. I can honestly and openly declare that...

I will leave a legacy!

A positively impactful one. And so can you! I challenge you to leave a legacy that many will remember you for in a great way. Even if you are doing something great in your community, I dare you to multiply your efforts.

I dare you to dream bigger. I petition you to make m oves so great that you begin to shock yourself! I believe in the gift in you to make that possible. You must believe....

# The Perfect Shade of Lipstick

BY JAIME A. GILL

Have you ever seen a woman in a jogging suit, very casual, maybe even a baseball cap on her head, with just her ponytail swinging in the back? There is nothing fancy about her. But then you see it, and for some reason, you can't stop staring at her. She has on the perfect shade of lipstick. It is not like you have never seen this color before, especially in lipstick, but it just compliments this woman so well.

The same can also be true with a woman in an evening gown. The "belle of the ball," the prettiest dress in the room— but let her have on a lipstick color that contrasts aggressively from her attire, or even her skin tone, and then suddenly, her overall look does not have the same effect as it would have if she would have chosen a different color or even no color at all. It amazes me how something so simple as lipstick can be the ultimate statement without saying a word.

There are many things in life, not just lipstick, that stand out but can stand alone, that are the perfect compliments to a given situation or outfit. I like to think of myself as lipstick.

## *I Am Lipstick*

There are many times during job interviews where potential employers will ask you, "if you were an inanimate object, what would you be and why?" These are questions that allow others to see how you see yourself. They want to know the things that you notice about yourself and how you evaluate your life, your skills, and even your weaknesses. My favorite answer is lipstick!

It is always a joy to see the look on the interviewer's face when they hear my response. Then they ask, "why lipstick?" To which my immediate response is, "why not!"

I have a love for lipstick and lip gloss. I would also beg my mom and grandmother to let me wear it. When they would get tired of me bothering them, they gave me chapstick. I would always explain it had no color and I needed something that "popped." It did not have to be a special occasion. I did not need to be dressed up. Lipstick was the exclamation point. It was the final thing needed to complete any look. The other cosmetics were nice, but I always thought they were not necessary. I deeply believed that all you needed was the right color lipstick.

In 2020, when the pandemic hit the world, it interrupted the ability for women to express their creativity with their lipsticks due to the mandate of wearing masks for our safety and the safety of others. Cosmetic companies capitalized on this and began rapidly creating matte and no-smear lipsticks. You can go to any cosmetic counter and see a wild array of colors and shades. There is red, "some like it hot" red, "go girl" red, "don't stop red", "ready or not red"...and the list goes on. How can a girl ever choose just one! But for each one, there is something that makes it stand out from the rest. Whether it's color, matte, moisturizer, sheer, cream, long-lasting, organic. Each characteristic and each purchaser's preference ultimately define what is the perfect lipstick shade.

I identify with this greatly because I always wanted my personal characteristics to allow me to stand out from the rest. I have always desired to be a person that can stand on my own, but when paired in the right situation, I am also the perfect compliment. Once I turned thirty-five, I realized that, as a woman, I was beginning to shift. For many women, throughout our lives, we are CONSISTENTLY asked when we are getting married or having children. As most young ladies do, we planned a perceived date, time, location, and color scheme of when we would like to be married with the entire wedding designed, bridesmaids picked out, and menu chosen. The only thing we were not certain about was who was going to be our handsome groom.

We dreamed of how many children we would have and what their names would be, and even picked out the hobbies they would have and the careers we wanted them to have. Now, although nothing is "wrong" with any of this, I began to realize that the same amount of questions were not coming to me about my passions, career goals, humanitarian efforts, philanthropic hopes, or even my mental or emotional health. Have we done a disservice to our girls by thinking that the only value they offer to the world is through the roles of wife or mother?

I realized that I had to redefine dating for myself. Let me preface this by saying that I am a fan and a supporter of both marriage and motherhood, but I am here to challenge that the list does not need to stop there. Now, as a forty-three year old woman, I am embracing the fact that I AM DOPE! If I make the decision to never get married or never have any children or adopt any children, I still have much to offer this world. I have been engaged and I have dated some good guys, but the question that I would always have to ask myself is, "Is this your assignment?" Not just the person, but the direction of the relationship. Often, as a woman, I would find in myself in a relationship because either that is what the man wanted or I felt that was what I was supposed to do. It was time, I was only getting older. I should "settle" down. That is exactly what I was doing...settling!

I had to sit down and ask myself some very serious and even life-changing questions. For me. this journey began when I had to have emergency surgery. My doctor found fibroid tumors, and the size of them concerned her. She did not know if the tumors were cancerous, and based on the location of the tumors, she did not know if it was going to jeopardize the prospect of me being able to have children. This news was a shock not just to my life and my health, but also from the perspective that I was in my thirties and, at the time, engaged. My then-fiancé made the statement that he would still love me if I couldn't have children, and he still wanted to marry me. Although that was nice to hear, that was not my concern at the time. My concern was how I was going to feel about myself. It is one thing to make the decision not to have a child; it is another to NOT BE ABLE TO!

I had to have a "come to Jesus meeting"—as I called it. I had to spend much time and prayer and self-reflection. I never thought about my life without children before that moment. In fact, I always wanted a very large family—a husband and five or six kids. Yes, even starting in my late 30s. I loved children and I got very excited about the idea of being pregnant—being a participant in the miracle of giving birth, raising a baby to hopefully become a really amazing person, and creating memories with my husband as we shared our life in creating a nurturing and loving environment for our children. Then suddenly this beautiful movie in my head came to an abrupt STOP! Fade to black! What would my life look like without kids???? Until that moment, I didn't even think that was an option.

Operation day came, and I had peace. I did not know what the outcome of the surgery was going to be. I didn't know what my life was going to look like or in what direction I was going to head once the anesthesia wore off, but I knew I wanted to live and be healthy and have the opportunity to figure it out. The operation was a success. Twenty-seven pounds of fibroid tumors were removed and NO CANCER! My doctor told me that everything went well, I'm fine, and I could "go forth and make babies." And I am sure my doctor thought that this statement would have made me very excited, but actually, it gave me mixed emotions. What my doctor did not realize is that by the time my actual surgery happened, I was no longer engaged or in that relationship. I had done so much spiritual and emotional work to prepare for the worst that I think I forgot to expect the best. I had prepared so much for the potential reality of not having children, it was like I could not process the thought of having them again.

It was then that I realized that sometimes we can have a plan so programmed in our head for our lives that we never consider another route. I realized at this moment that I did not want the success of my life to only be defined by the titles of wife and mother....I didn't want my relationship status to be the reason that my very life meant anything....I wanted my value to be because I was JAIME. I could still offer many gifts to the world. I wanted to be an author. I wanted to create meaningful content that would inspire the world. I wanted to take care of my parents. I wanted to mentor and encourage young people. I wanted to build stronger relationships with my family and have amazing adventures with my friends. I wanted to stand out and be the perfect lipstick

## *I Can...*

"I can" is such a powerful phrase. It alludes to having the ability to or the permission to. I can do. I can be. This phrase, with words following or just the two words alone, speaks power. I can be! I can do!

I wanted to reexamine my life to align it with what God wanted and CREATED ME to do and to be. In the Bible, the book of the Apostle Paul talks about how everything is permissible but not everything is beneficial (1 Corinthians 10:23). Meaning I CAN DO whatever I choose to do, but just because I chose it does not mean it is the best thing for me. I CAN eat two gallons of ice cream. But I am pretty sure it would make me sick to do that. I CAN go driving down the street with my eyes closed. Not only is that dangerous, but it is reckless, and I will injure myself or others. Evaluating what you can and cannot do as it relates to your decision-making ability should not be the ultimate determinant of if you SHOULD actually do something.

This thought process became my evaluation model as I was approaching forty and definitely AFTER I turned forty....I am sure we all have thoughts and dreams for our life and a timetable of which we would like to have some things accomplished. There were many things that I thought I would have accomplished by a certain time, and at the same time, there were a lot of things that I had accomplished that I never even imagined. Being able to film a wedding in the Bahamas, having an opportunity to have produced broadcast internationally, the opportunity to have worked in hospitality, media, education...all things I could have never imagined. Blessings!

Throughout my career, it has amazed me just how much I am asked about my personal life and goals outside of my career. As a leader and manager, I can recognize the power of knowing how personal goals align with the professional to see if a person is a quality candidate that would be compatible for their team. I have never had a problem describing or discussing my goals, but I can't help but think about the people/women who have a problem talking about this area. What if they are having difficulty finding love? What if they are unable to conceive or have no desire to have a child or husband? Is this woman now deemed "unfit" because of her reality/choice? Can a single woman with no children work for a family-focused company? OF COURSE SHE CAN!!! Just because she doesn't have or doesn't desire does not mean that she cannot create the environment for healthy growth and opportunity for others.

I can! I can build a beautiful, successful career and be a positive influence in the world because my community becomes my family. My time is just as available, if not more. Now, I have a family...my mom, siblings, extended family, and my friends... this is my family. My relationships and connections with them will naturally pull and have demand that I manage—we all do! No two people's lives are identical. The thing that brings me so much peace and, honestly, joy is that...

## *I Will...*

Today, I am a single woman with no children and I am happy and at peace. I don't know what I will be in the future. When I am asked if I have a desire to be married or have children, my automatic answer is—I only want what God wants for me! I am truly learning to let Jesus take the wheel. I have tried to be in control of so much in my life that I think that I have missed a lot and spent time in spaces that I should have never been in or been in so long.

I was at a conference for young people that I emceed where there was a huge white tarp that said at the top, "Before I die..." Attendees were instructed to write down something we wanted to do in our lifetime. As I stood before this huge tarp that covered over twenty feet of floor space, I saw young people share so many of their dreams, hopes, plans. As I stood there, I thought about what things I wanted to do before I died. There were things that I definitely wanted to do, and then there were things that I would like to do, but did not carry the same weight of importance to me.

As I get older, each day, I think about that tarp...those students...their dreams...mine! There are many plans and dreams that have changed. They didn't change because they didn't happen; they changed because I changed. I am happy to say that if I never get married or have a child, I WILL LIVE A FULFILLING LIFE. I wake up everyday with the opportunity to dream and actively pursue each dream. I have the gift of my mother being alive and experiencing life with her. Helping her to live her best life and fulfill her retirement dream to "walk on the beach and dance in the streets." My focus used to be to get the fancy job with the fancy title, a corner office overlooking downtown. Now I desire different things. I want to be able to take the gifts that God has given me along with the skills I have developed over the years to be able to positively make an impact in people's lives. I want to encourage women to realize their value and embrace their lives fully. I want them to stop apologizing for their desires as well as their emotions. I want men to know that it is OK for them to be vulnerable. I want young people to embrace their youth and hone their skills and recognize they can be leaders NOW and later! I want people to be in HEALTHY PRODUCTIVE RELATIONSHIPS that make both parties better! I want people to have a life that they dream and work hard for, that compliments them in the best way...not for a life that they settle for because of habit, the fear of being alone or judged, or a false sense of security.

I will be lipstick! I will stand boldly and bright alone, and I will also compliment my assigned situations. The love I have for life will not be limited only to my relationship status and what my womb can produce. Each of us has an assignment in life. To be and fully manifest that which we were created to be and do. I will make sure that with every remaining breath in my body, I will explore every given opportunity to discover all of what that is! I will live unapologetically, love boldly and be ONLY THAT WHICH I WAS CREATED. No longer do I crave the life and assignment meant for others. My deepest desire is to DIE EMPTY—coloring the world with the bold, vibrant, long-lasting lipstick intensity that I AM!

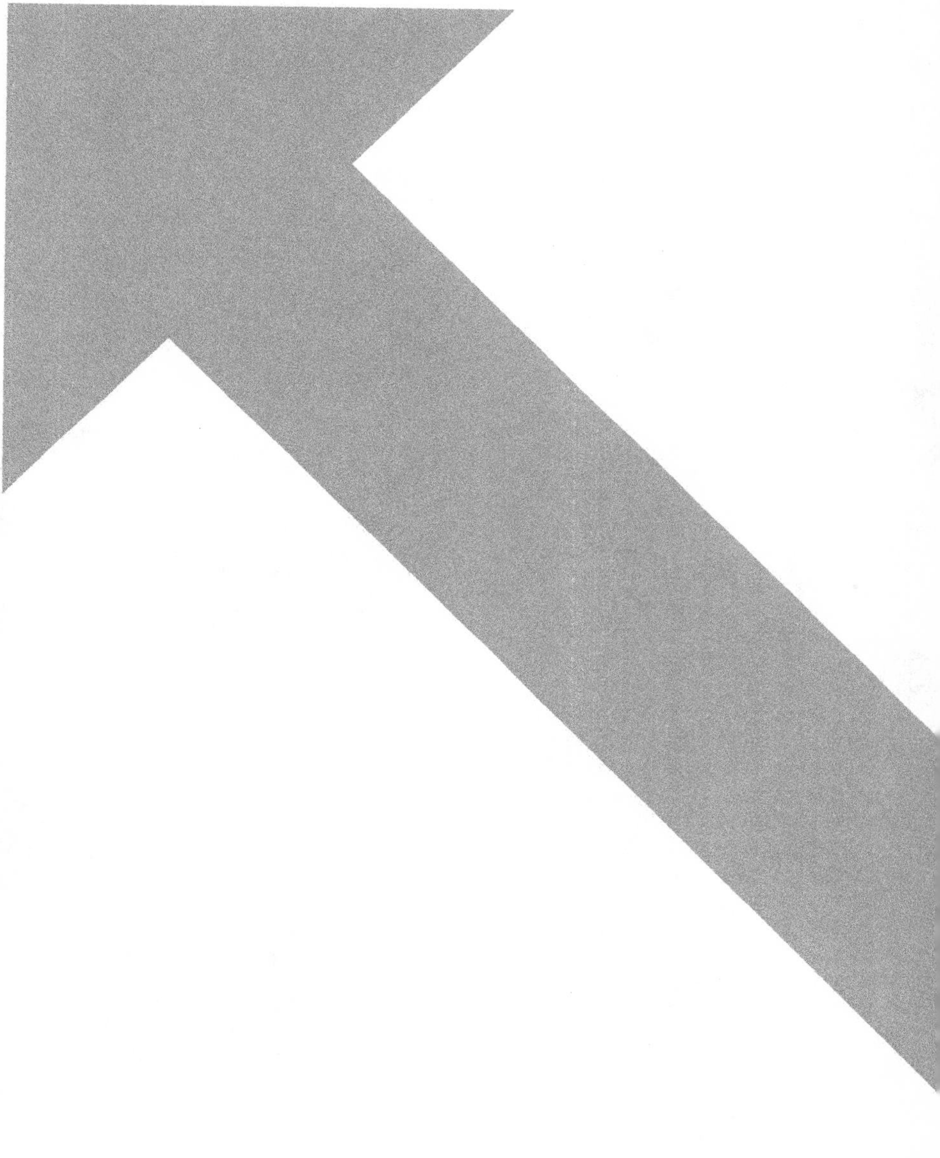

Printed in the USA
CPSIA information can be obtained
at www.ICGtesting.com
LVHW042307151123
763951LV00022B/16